SEEDS OF FAITH

Gratitude

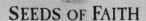

SEEDS OF FAITH

Gratitude

Words of Faith from
NORMAN VINCENT PEALE

Ideals Publications · Nashville, Tennessee

ISBN 0-8249-4646-4

Published by Ideals Publications, a division of Guideposts
535 Metroplex Drive, Suite 250, Nashville, Tennessee 37211
www.idealsbooks.com

Editor, Peggy Schaefer
Designer, Marisa Calvin
Cover photograph: Pixtal/SuperStock
Interior photographs by age fotostock/SuperStock. Photo page 3 by
Pixtal/Superstock.

Printed and bound in Mexico by RR Donnelley
10 9 8 7 6 5 4 3 2 1

ACKNOWLEDGMENTS
All scripture quotations, unless otherwise noted, are taken from The
King James Version of the Bible.

Do not always *ask* when you pray,
but instead affirm that God's blessings
are being given and spend most
of your prayer giving thanks.

—NORMAN VINCENT PEALE

FOREWORD

Throughout his long career, my father, Norman Vincent Peale, valued no message more than that of the importance of faith in each of our lives. In fact, before the title was finalized, *The Power of Positive Thinking* was called *The Power of Faith*. It was that important to him.

Growing up in the Midwest at the beginning of the twentieth century, Dad learned about faith at his parents' knees and in the pews of small-town churches. Faith in God, country, and fellow man, and the saving message of Jesus Christ filled his youthful days. He learned oratorical skills by listening to the great preachers of the day,

who went from town to town, bringing countless people to faith. He became filled with faith messages, and they never left him.

When the personal call came for him to enter the ministry, Dad was well equipped with deep faith, a gift for communicating, and a love of people. His writings were full of anecdotes of the faith journeys of countless people he met along the way. By their examples, he was able to lead others to a life of faith. His was a great calling, and I think we can all agree that he succeeded.

As you read, I hope you enjoy the messages in this book and that it brings deeper faith into your life.

—*Elizabeth Peale Allen*

O give thanks unto the LORD; for he is good; for his mercy endureth forever.

—PSALM 106:1

One of the great principles of life is that of thanksgiving. Not only is giving thanks a recognition of past benefits, it is the activator of blessings yet to come. As the experiences of many people demonstrate, thankfulness activates a continuous flow of blessings. If in your life there is a paucity of blessings, it just might be that your tendency to thankfulness has grown weak and inactive. But as we practice thanksgiving, assiduously and constantly, we can develop a deep joy in living, even though life may be filled with all manner of suffering and difficulty.

I'm afraid most of us are deficient in the practice of thanksgiving, except on rare occasions. I've observed, however, that the people who live the most joyously live in what you might call a constant "attitude of gratitude." They are astonished and delighted, and receive the blessings of life with a sense of wonder.

The idea of systematically practicing thanksgiving is hardly original with me. Actually, it came to me from a man who regularly attended Marble Collegiate Church in the latter years of his life. One day, as he was chatting with me in my study, he talked about this idea: if a person would each day deliberately practice thanksgiving, he would activate new sources of energy and power within him. He stood up before me—straight and tall, a very alive and obviously healthy man even in his nineties—and said, "Every day of my life, when I rise in the morning, I do my exercises and my deep breathing, and then I say a prayer and give thanks to God for my good body.

"The body," he continued, "is a wonderful instrument. Think of the skill that went into the making of its intricate, interrelated parts and functions! When it works well, it is a thing of beauty and a joy forever. And one of the ways to make it work well is to affirm it as efficient.

"So," he said, "I start at my head and I run down through my whole body: I give thanks to God for my two eyes that bring the world into my awareness. I thank God for my good digestion. I thank God for my joints, that they work freely and

without inhibition. I thank God for the temple of the soul, and for the effectiveness of its operation over these many years."

I stood looking at this man over ninety years of age, the picture of health, and had a new sense of gratitude and respect for the physical body, the temple of the soul, created by the good God.

It's a simple law: if you affirm goodness, goodness will follow; if you affirm love, love will be there; if you affirm thankfulness, blessings will come. Many intelligent people diligently follow this principle. I once read a newspaper article about a dear old friend of mine who had passed away. Everyone

Gratitude is the
memory of the heart.
JEAN BAPTISTE MASSIEU

loved him. And he had been richly blessed all his life. According to the article, his last will and testament was found to contain the following declaration:

I desire to testify and give thanks for the goodness of God, who has blessed me far beyond my merit; for Godly parents; for the patience and devotion of my wife; for the Christian character, love, and loyalty of my darling daughter, my son-in-law, and their family, my grandchildren; the rich fellowship of my friends; the kindness and cooperation of those with whom I have been associated in business; the opportunities for service in the community and in the church; the strength for daily toil; the joy of living; the

inexpressible reward of striving, even in an imperfect way, to follow Christ, and the glorious certainty of life eternal and abundant. These comprise my real possessions.

It isn't every day that one hears of a last will and testament in which it appears that the principal objective of the deceased was to give thanks for the real blessings of this life. I think I know why my friend had so many blessings. He was constantly activating the flow of blessings by giving thanks to the Source of it all. If you want to keep the blessings coming, a good way to begin is by giving praise and thanks to Almighty God this day.

$\mathcal{I}$n the book of 1 Thessalonians we find these words: "In every thing give thanks: for this is the will of God in Christ Jesus concerning you" (1 Thessalonians 5:18). I would take this to mean that in everything—things that seem hopeful or things that seem difficult—it is the will of God that we be thankful. Both spiritually and mentally, thankfulness, which is really an affirmation of God's goodness, works to our benefit and tends to let loose untold blessings in our lives. If we emphasize that which is possible through Jesus Christ and are hopeful rather than dwelling on the difficult, good things tend to come to pass. This does not imply that we are to be blind to the difficulties, the injustice, or the pain in human existence; but we are to thank God always that by His grace and power we can come to better days.

"What is there to be thankful for?" This phrase was thrown at me one night in Switzerland by a very disgruntled American. This gentleman had tried to go to church that morning, but had been frustrated. It was the Swiss Thanksgiving Day,

Now therefore, our God,
we thank thee, and praise
thy glorious name.

1 CHRONICLES 29:13

which falls on a Sunday; and, to his exasperation, he had found every church filled to capacity.

We were seated on a hotel terrace in Interlaken. The sky was star-studded; the light from a full moon was filling the night. We were surrounded by beauty on every hand, but this man was letting loose a veritable tirade. "Why did all those people go to church to give thanks?" he wanted to know. "All thanksgiving is phony. There isn't anything to be thankful for."

And he proceeded to enumerate the many negatives that obviously had been haunting his mind. He dwelt at length upon tight money, which would ultimately, he said, choke our economy. He had much to say about what he called "give-away government and confiscatory taxes." He went on and on, giving reasons why there was nothing to be thankful for. "Why," he grumbled, "I even go to church, or try to, and I can't get a seat!"

Just then the clouds pulled away from a nearby mountaintop and it stood out, shining and silver and glorious against the night. I looked at my companion and he was silent for a moment. Then he admitted, "Well, maybe there are a few things in this world for which we should thank God."

I thought the conversation had taken its proper

turn and let it ride at that point. But he returned to deploring the fact that the world was full of tumult, with all kinds of conflict everywhere. "Why can't we have a world that is peaceful and quiet?" he complained.

I told him about an old Irish preacher I once knew who said that some in Ireland believed that when there is trouble on the earth, it means there is movement in heaven. This old preacher used to say, "I always rejoice when there's lots of conflict and upset on earth, because I know that, out of the movement, in heaven a greater world is coming to pass."

"Well," my friend remarked, "it could just be."

23

In every thing . . . That's difficult, but that's the admonition. "In every thing give thanks: for this is the will of God in Christ Jesus concerning you."

One of the greatest of the early American philosophers, and for that matter one of the greatest American philosophers of all time, was Henry David Thoreau. As far as anybody has been able to ascertain, he never traveled more than fifty miles from his home at Concord, Massachusetts.

The distinguishing thing about Thoreau is that he thought his own thoughts. He did not mimic anybody's else's thoughts; he was an original thinker. Therefore, while unoriginal thinkers of his day

One single grateful
thought raised to
heaven is the
most perfect prayer.

G. E. LESSING

have fallen into oblivion with the passing of time, Thoreau's wisdom still influences the country whose thinking he helped to formulate.

One of the wise things this thinker said was that every human being ought to give thanks at least once every day for the fact that he was born. Thoreau said that he did this himself.

Just think what you would have missed had you never been born. I've heard some people say that they wished they hadn't been born; but they do not really mean it. That is only a reaction to difficulty. So we repeat: Just think what you would have missed had you never been born. Why, pull yourself up tall and thank the good God that He let you be born!

Of course, there is always somebody around to argue, "But how can you be thankful for life in a day and age like this? Just look at all the difficulties that beset us!" Well, God allowed those difficulties to develop because He wanted us to grow, and that is a pretty tough job. He gave us the opportunity to struggle in life. The thrill of it makes you want to say the second verse of the 103rd Psalm: "Bless the LORD, O my soul, and forget not all his benefits." Reduced to common English speech, this means to thank God and be sure that you do not forget all that He has done for you.

What is there to be thankful for? Surely we should be thankful for the love-light in the eyes of a wife or husband, the curling of little fingers around our own. We should be thankful for home on a cold winter night, with welcoming lights and a fire in the fireplace. Think of the many beautiful nights, with the moon shining between bare branches of the trees; the aroma of burning leaves in autumn; the fragrance of honeysuckle in the springtime; the crunch of snow in the winter. Be thankful for health and vitality and strength. These are common things that we do not ordinarily emphasize, but they are real reasons for thanksgiving.

*O*ftentimes I have heard beauty in prayer. But my thought is now directed to a gentleman who was in a meeting not so long ago where folks were talking about various difficulties and problems, both in our society and as individuals. The group called upon this man to pray. Now, I knew that he had had much difficulty and was even then having a lot; so I was astonished by his prayer. He did not

Unto thee, O God, do we give thanks, unto thee do we give thanks . . .

PSALM 75:1

ask the Lord, as far as I can recall, for a single thing except His presence. And he quickly affirmed this presence. The prayer was full of thanksgiving and of affirmation of God's loving kindness and goodness. It was an entrancing prayer; and I said to him, "Jim, I suppose I shouldn't comment on a prayer, but I'm intrigued by the one you just offered. All you did in it was give thanks and affirm God's loving kindness. I know something of the difficulties you face. How come you never ask God for anything?"

"Oh," he replied, "I've learned that the best way to pray is to thank God. He knows what I need.

So I just thank Him because He's Himself." Then he added, with a somewhat surprised look, "Why should I ask Him for anything? Let me just tell you all the wonderful things I have." And he began to enumerate his blessings. No matter how much difficulty you have—and there may be lots—he emphasized that you still have many, many things for which to be thankful.

There came to my mind the thought that thanks givers equate with blessing receivers. I believe it is a law of human life that there's a correlation between inner attitudes and outer manifestations. That is to say, what we are within ourselves we tend to have or create outside us. For example, if your mind is full of hate and resentment and ill will and grudges, you can be sure that you will manifest these things in the life outside your inner soul. We activate what we think. If you're filled with fear, anxiety, worry, apprehension, you manifest these things so that your life becomes one of fear and anxiety.

Or, let us say, you constantly think in terms of scarcity. Now this is perhaps a little more difficult to grasp, but I have observed that people who think scarcity tend, in a strange way, to manifest scarcity. The word *scarcity* is related to the word *scarce*. And there is only one letter's difference between *scarce* and *scare*. It could be that if you think scarcity, you scare money and prosperity away. This is, as I say, a little harder to demonstrate than the other correlations between attitudes and outcomes; but you might consider trying it out. Instead of saying, "How difficult everything is for me; how poor I am," affirm how God is helping you, how blessed you are. Avoid manifesting scarcity by thinking scarcity thoughts.

By the same token, if in our minds we entertain thanksgiving, we manifest blessings. The more thankfulness a person cultivates, the more, I

Gratitude is not only the
greatest of virtues, but the
parent of all others.

CICERO

believe, he will open to himself the power flow, the vast wealth of heaven, and blessings will pour out upon him.

$\mathcal{T}$here is a great art to living in simple gratitude to God. A big trouble with many of us is that we keep adding up in our minds all the things that are bad. The human mind is conditioned this way—we have no trouble at all telling ourselves or other people how many troubles we have. But there is a solution to this problem.

I think Walter Huston, the great actor, was asked one time what, in his opinion, was the greatest sentence in the English language. And he said, "It's from an old Negro spiritual: 'Nobody knows the troubles I've seen. Glory Hallelujah!'" That is to say, we sure have plenty of trouble, but we also have an answer to it, which is "Glory Hallelujah!" Instead of saying to yourself that this is bad and that is bad, the thing to do is to add up your blessings, fix your mind on the things that are good and on the opportunities you have, and then give thanks in simple gratitude to God.

"Well," you say, "it's all very well for you to tell

me that. But you don't know the troubles I have."
Don't I? Well, you ought to read my mail. But from
time to time I have received some very marvelous,
very inspiring letters.

A woman once wrote to me from upstate New
York, enclosing a copy of some reflections written
by a fourteen-year-old girl. This girl was as full of
life as any fourteen-year-old girl. But at the age of
six she had been stricken with infantile paralysis
and it left her so crippled that physically she was
practically helpless, unable to sit and having only
partial use of her hands. Yet at fourteen she was
maintaining tenth-grade studies.

*Thanks be unto God
for his unspeakable gift.*

2 CORINTHIANS 9:15

She could have kept adding up the bad things and filled her mind with self-pity, but she didn't. As you read what she has written, ask yourself if you could write these things.

I think that without a doubt I am the luckiest person in the world, and here are the reasons why:

I was given the most marvelous thing of all—the gift of life—and with it, the ability to reason right from wrong and to remember all the happy moments of yesterday and to dream of the possibilities of tomorrow.

I was given two ears so that I may hear the lovely sound of the brook, the happy song of a robin on a spring day, and the sound of rain as it cleanses and moistens the thirsty earth, giving to all things new life.

I was blessed with the gift of sight, so that I am able to see the great beauties of nature. I had the fortune of being born in a country where beauty is boundless and we have the bluest sky, the greenest grass, and the brightest sun in the world.

But I don't see always with my eyes; I see with my heart too. As I look around me on a summer day or on a winter day, I know that God is near me; for I see Him in every flower and in every blade of grass and in every snowflake that drifts across our lawn.

I have the most wonderful and understanding parents who ever lived. And if I regret mistakes I made today, there is always the gift of another tomorrow, a new beginning. I make a secret vow in my heart that tomorrow I will better myself, be a little more understanding, a little kinder, and thus make myself worthy of the many blessings God has so graciously bestowed upon me.

The woman who wrote to me says this young girl "has the face of an angel." That is undoubtedly because—judging from her words about her life—she has the soul of a hero.

$\mathscr{I}$ would like to emphasize once more that what you have in your attitude affects what happens. If your attitude is one of gratitude, it will result in blessings abundantly received.

I will close with the example of a man with whom I talked not long ago. This man wanted to speak with me because he had experienced, as he put it, one tragedy after another in his life. He quoted to me that passage from Shakespeare's *Hamlet* which says, "When sorrows come, they

Hem your blessings with thankfulness so they don't unravel.

AUTHOR UNKNOWN

come not single spies, / But in battalions." And this is often true. To use a more common phrase, we may say, "Sometimes life throws the whole book at you." That is what had happened to this man. He said, "I want you to tell me whether I'm handling this situation as a Christian should." Then he told me how he was handling it: "I've made a list of all my problems and difficulties. Alongside it I've made a list of my blessings. Now, when I started to make these lists, I thought the difficulties would completely overtop the blessings. But just look, just look at my list of blessings! Isn't it wonderful how good God is?

"So," he told me, "I have been praying this way: 'Lord, thank You for all You've done for me and all You've given me and for all that You are. The only thing I ask of You is that You help me with my difficulties as You think best.'"

And again he asked me, "Do you think that is the way a Christian should handle it?"

I replied, "You are a thanks giver and you will be a blessings receiver."

The Bible tells us in the book of Colossians, "Let the peace of God rule in your hearts . . . and be ye thankful" (Colossians 3:15).

Have you had a hard time this past year? The

Scripture tells us you should give thanks for it. Hard times, struggled with in the name of Jesus, become victories by and by, and we are stronger people for the tussling. Have you had sorrow? Bereavement? Through your tears, give thanks for it; for it is through difficult circumstances that souls grow. Whatever life has brought, the message is: Give thanks. And, as you do so, greater things will come.

Remember Psalm 103:2: "Bless the LORD, O my soul, and forget not all his benefits." Do not be unmindful of the simple everyday blessings God showers upon you. If you practice thanksgiving, joy and satisfaction will be engendered in your life and will contribute to the happiness of all those who touch your life.